MOTIVATING YOUR MENTAL MUSCLE

Kedesha Dallas Goode

**Empowerment Conversations: Motivating your Mental Muscle
by Kedesha Dallas Goode**

All scripture quotations, unless otherwise indicated, are taken from the Holy Bible, the New King James Version

ISBN: 978-1-949343-47-2

Front & back cover design: Dionne R. Ramdeen
Book Design, Layout, Typesetting & Formatting: Dionne R. Ramdeen
Tel: (876) 339-2981
Email: dionnerachaelcreative@gmail.com
Instagram: @dionnerachaelcreative
Website: https://dionnerachael.wixsite.com/creative

Books may be purchased by contacting the author, Kedesha Dallas Goode, at
Website: www.kdallasgoode.com
Tel: 876.822.5634
Facebook: Kedesha Dallas Goode
Email: kdallasgoode@gmail.com
Instagram: @kedgoode | @creativegoodenesshub
Online: www.amazon.com

Dedication

To the dreamers of the impossible, the believers of the unattainable and the doers of the undoable, I dedicate these conversations to you. I hope the book's content will add a consistent element of vim, vigour and vitality to your purpose and passions. Put God first place. He'll ensure that you'll not only run your race, but also finish with style and grace, when you believe.

TABLE OF CONTENTS

Foreword

Conversations have the ability to open reciprocal and transparent communication that is somewhat informal and relaxing. Conversations are meaningful when all parties involved can express themselves in a space where there is a single chord of individual and collective fulfillment. In my quest to: maintain my mental strength, mind my mental wellness and build my mental muscle, I was blessed with the idea of Empowerment Conversations©. The single concise objective is to empower our minds to reliably govern our actions knowing that God is the CEO of all our affairs and He can do what His words say. All we are required to do is – *BELIEVE*.

The New Year crept upon me with its overwhelming standards of achievement urgency that surfaced questions of resolutions, and a lot of 'what next?' Plans to proceed among many others. Like many of us, I felt stuck in the mundane plans of a scroll of New Year declarations that sparked a whole lot of talk and little action. On the heels of my introspective start to the year, these conversations were birthed. They are in no way fictitious or fad infused, instead they are real issues based on real conversations that I have with family, friends and myself. We all are facing some harsh realities; we are all on a journey towards self-fulfillment, purpose and prosperity. However, on this path we become wrapped up in a myriad of feelings that can quickly snowball to create pandemonium.

If we are not careful to maintain a made up mind we will crumble into fear and doubt; crush into self-pity; and cram ourselves with people's expectations and opinions. It is not an overnight accomplishment or a quick triumph but it's worth a try. When you stay on top of life's problems and challenges with daily and intentional affirmations that detour you from 'doom and gloom' street towards the avenue of endless possibilities, consistent efforts and purposeful actions, you will overcome and conquer.

As Romans 8:37 that declares–"in all these things we are more than conquerors through Him that loves us."

On a Prayer Path ...
Victory, Progress, Success!

1 John 5:14
This is the confidence we have in approaching God, that if we ask anything according to His will, he hears us...**NKJV**

> **Think about it ...**
> **Confidence** - *Trust, Faith, Belief in ...*
> **God's Will** - *Has Reason & Purpose, Strategically Crafted...*

Jeremiah 29:11
For I know the plans I have for you declares the Lord, plans to prosper you and not to harm you, plans to give you hope and a future. **NKJV**

Ephesians 6:18
Praying always with all prayer and supplication in the spirit, being watchful to this end with all perseverance and supplication for all the saints. **NKJV**

Everybody wants to have a story in victory; everybody wants a piece of progress, and everybody wants to achieve success. **And you ask yourself. What's the stress?!**

Wanting it and working for it go hand in hand; they both require intentional and consistent commitment. If you want something and want it really bad, you have to be tough enough to conquer the pessimistic extrinsic elements. *They are inevitable, a consistently positive attitude is to PRAY !*

A dream starts with a vision, a hope and a desire to materialize that which you cannot yet touch. You cannot want it and not even wish for it! The moment you realize you have a God given purpose and/or talent, start step one. PRAY without ceasing! Dedicate some solid time to prayer, seek out God's guidance and direction, and tap into the quiet moments of your heart so you can listen to yourself wanting to succeed; so that you can 'put some pep' in your steps to create the success that you crave.

KEDESHA DALLAS GOODE

That success which seems unattainable which really is within reach, if you pray with grit and without ceasing.

Communing with God creates clarity so that He will order your steps. Instead of being victimized and distracted by everybody's dreams for you, focus on your forward flow. Do not refuse to fight with prayer, fight means stand up and challenge God, challenge Him to fulfill His promises in you. You have to own your prayer!

Let your requests be made known to God and allow Him direct you. When you become inexplicably tired of waiting, pray some more, when you become tired of praying stay committed to the promise that God will make a way! Hold on! The right time, the right opportunity and the right attitude to receive your breakthrough will come! Be tough to wait and watch how you act while waiting.

> **⁶Be anxious for nothing, but in everything by prayer and supplication, with thanksgiving, let your requests be made known to God; ⁷and the peace of God, which surpasses all understanding, will guard your hearts and minds through Christ Jesus.**
>
> **- Phillipians 4:6-7**

Pump up your Prayer!

Pray! Not if you may!
Pray because it is the most effective way!
God didn't say
He'll try …
For as true as the night
Is to day,
So His words will not stray!
He will make a way!
So …
Pray night,
Pray day,
Pray, pray, pray!
Pump up your prayer,
Reject the naysayer.
Amplify your energy,
Create a synergy with
The almighty!
Power up your prayer,
To accommodate,
Your elevate.
Why wait?
Make it a date!
To PRAY,
Before it's too late!

Your Aim — The Mountain Top. Are You Willing to Climb?

Proverbs 19:21
There are many plans in a man's heart, Nevertheless the Lord's counsel – that will stand. **NKJV**

Think about it...
A Process - *A series of action/steps taken to achieve a specific end.*
God's Purpose - *Established plan for our lives that must be accomplished.*

Job 42:2
I know that You can do everything, and that no purpose of Yours can be withheld from You. **NKJV**

Hebrews 10:36
For you have need of endurance, so that after you have done the will of God, you may receive the promise. **NKJV**

You plan to visit YS Falls, you are super thrilled because it's your first time there.

The Purpose = YS FALLS.
The Process = Driving to an unknown part of the country.

If you could blink your eyes and arrive at your location, wouldn't that be great? Your purpose would require no hassle, and you would be instantly gratified. What process? The reality is there is a process!

The process involves: patience, excitement, discovery, will power, rest, anxiety and responsibility. Everybody wants to be attached to a purpose and of course we all have a purpose, but never forget there is a journey to achieve that purpose and it's the…PROCESS!

While your purpose may sometimes be clear in your mind, the process can be daunting! Everybody wants to get to the mountain top, but dread the climb. Why?!

That's because the process (of gaining anything) requires so much out of us than the achievement of the PURPOSE itself. The strongest yet hardest characteristic that hovers over us is PATIENCE! Whether we like it or not, we have to wait.

Waiting erupts a volcano of emotions that range from:
- Happiness to know that we have discovered our purpose;
- Expectation of the best outcome;
- Disruption fuelled by unpredictable disappointments;
- Anger due to impatience and uncertainty;
- Fluctuating faith because of what cannot be seen as it is perceived in the mind.

The beauty of the process is, it manifests the true substance of the purpose. The moment you recognize the lessons of each experience (good or bad) connected to the process, is the point in your personal growth that you will discover–mental muscle. It has to be strengthened with positive dumbbells consistently pumping tenacity and push into your being so that anger and frustration will not derail or demotivate your ability to reach your destination–the purpose.

When you recognize your purpose, pay attention to the hills and valleys of the process so that your attitude will not stunt your progress towards your purpose. You cannot accomplish the purpose without going through the process. True faith is praising God while you are heading to the destination (your purpose) because it is, indeed, easier to praise God when you get what you have always wanted. Don't allow bitter to overwhelm better; don't let anger prevail over wisdom. God's will must be fulfilled in your life. Pay attention to the Process!

**The P in Process & Purpose –
P U S H!**

Don't you want to achieve
Your goal?
You have a purpose
You're told,
But as life unfolds,
Your efforts grow cold,
What purpose?!
Like the disfigured mould,
Your purpose pursuits,
Have become old,
Old and gray,
But, it is a new day!
Recognize the road
To your destination,
Analyze every situation,
Push through the process,
Disappointments,
Distractions, there's no recess!
You cannot win,
If your patience hasn't
Worn thin,
The experience
Manifests resilience,
Push! It will be worth the recompense!

How can you relate to this month's issue?

KEDESHA DALLAS GOODE

Falling in Failure
Or ... Forward in Faith

Psalms 73:26

My flesh and my heart fail; but God is the strength of my heart and my portion forever. **NKJV**

Think about it …
Faith - Complete trust or confidence in someone or something.
Failure - Lack of success; the neglect or omission of expected or required action.

Philippians 4:13

I can do all things through Christ who strengthens me. **NKJV**

Romans 8:18

For I consider that the sufferings of this present time are not worthy to be compared with the glory which shall be revealed in us. **NKJV**

They say encouragement sweetens labour. In the same way, wouldn't visibility sweeten faith? Oh yes! Absolutely! Imagine this—two hot cups of tea, one with sugar and the other without. Then picture someone who despises the idea of drinking tea but has to. His or her encouragement or motivation for gulping down that tea is knowing that the sweetener would give it a more appealing taste.

Now picture someone who loves tea but has to drink it to help with some sickness, and after constantly drinking, nothing much happens. In this case the avid tea drinker would be encouraged by some positive proof that their labour will not fail. Both scenarios exemplify some amount of failure and require a lot of faith. Increased faith means failure is imminent but your growth is consistent.

The aroma of failure is just not enough ammunition to increase your faith. However, a taste of failure whether

KEDESHA DALLAS GOODE

once, twice or too much to handle is the strong wind beneath your wings to soar your faith to another level. Have you ever hoped for something so badly that upon starting the journey, you purpose in your mind that no matter what, tenacity and resilience will govern your thoughts and actions. However, unpredictable failure and/or disappointments can totally discombobulate your hope of achieving the unattainable; your feelings–frustration, despair, and a pensive pessimistic trance of hopelessness. At this crossroads, but wait–there is actually no road, only dead ends! It seems. Nevertheless, you HAVE TO TRY–shake the stress, ward off the worry, dismiss depression and grab hold of the grit to go forward in spite of…God expects us to fail sometimes. That is why His grace and mercies are sufficient refuge references through which we are guaranteed comfort to know that if we believe He'll take care of us. HE WILL!

Even when you feel as if your strength is worn thin and you just cannot go on, you must brave the stormy seasons and hold on to the truth that God is our refuge and strength; a very present help in trouble. It's so hard! I know! Don't give in to the devil's games, Get up and CONQUER!

Failure forces our efforts to freeze; Faith flourishes our fight to go forward.

Faith OR Failure

I've come to know about this faith thing …
Only because I really want to win,
Really! Win? Win at what?
You have to start so some of your efforts can get shot!
But why shot?
Being shot, and shot, and shot
Shows you what stamina and grit you've got!
And, so I start to exercise faith, But I can't see what I want,
Faith says trust and feel what you want and soon you'll
begin to see what people can't!
Failure surfaces, so I start to feel that after all this faith thing
isn't real.
My feelings of faith have become frail,
My faith – derail,
Failure – prevail,
My Life's journey has become this tug-of-war tale,
Wait! God promised my faith wont become stale, so I
believe and trust because my victory won't be contained!

How can you relate to this month's issue?

EMPOWERMENT CONVERSATIONS

Let Your Light Shine,
In the Stark Dark ...

John 8:12
Then Jesus spoke…"I am the light of the world. He who follows Me shall not walk in darkness, but have the light of life." **NKJV**

Think about it…
Light - *The natural agent that stimulates sight and makes things visible.*
Darkness - *The (total) absence or deficiency of light.*

Psalm 119:105
Your word is lamp to my feet, and a light to my path. **NKJV**

John 12:35
Then Jesus said to them, "a little while longer the light is with you. Walk while you have the light, lest darkness overtake you; he who walks in darkness does not know where he is going." **NKJV**

Sun-light is very powerful. It is said to be able to light up the ocean up to 80 metres. Darkness, on the other hand, blocks the light from the sun and forms a shadow. Who wants to be associated with the gloom of darkness when the radiance of light is so dominant and effective?

Is there a light inside of you? Do you feel like the outer darkness of life influenced by harsh realities are dimming your light? How can you keep your light blazing even when everything seems to be hopelessly dark around you? Darkness dampens your hopes of making possibilities visible. Light brightens your path to victory. When you experience the love of God through Jesus Christ, you will have light even in your darkest hour(s).

Do you want to be a potent illuminator or just a mere shadow?

Dark moments in your life can be very unbearable, unpredictable, inexplicable and simply damaging to your strength of character. Have you ever been so deeply locked into the darkness of a situation that you cannot possibly imagine any light of deliverance and hope? In your mind, your options are limited, or so the dark situation makes you feel. So how do you find your light? What do you do? Drown in darkness and sorrow, prance in pity and conclude that there's no brighter tomorrow? Solid, positive and consistent self-affirmations are effective tools that can combat the dejection you feel when you're at a dark place. What should you tell yourself?

GOD is bigger than all my fears, doubts, insecurities, uncertainties and worries. I am built to conquer, not to cower in fear. There is a light inside of me; I won't zoom the gloom, I will overcome the hurdles. I will focus on MY dreams, stay in MY lane, run MY race and celebrate MY accomplishments no matter how small I think they are.

The Bible affirms that weeping may endure for a night but joy comes in the morning. Sometimes my night is long, dark, tiresome and frustrating! Do you experience this too? Thankfully the "but" breaks the spell and assures that joy will come–a breakthrough must manifest itself.

Just hold on and believe! You better hold on, you better believe, you better try your best to persevere because you will not crumble and be crushed. You have the viable option to tap into your uncanny ability to overthrow life's sometimes bitter blows.

Amidst the dark moments, what blessings can you look to so that you will recognize the light that stlll exists? Think on this…Give thanks.

Shine Your Light

You were born with a light
Yes, there is a light!
As life skips from day to night,
Shining your light
Is a constant fight,
You are plagued by the parasites
That keep diming your light,
Your mind propels you,
Shine! Shine bright!
Don't give up, don't give in,
Shine, shine, shine bright.
Hmnn … You might
Consider if the fight,
Is worth making your
Heavy load light?
Life's loads crush you,
They devour you, sometimes
They overpower you,
Yes you do! Yes you do!
Have the power in you.
You are made up of different hues
Shine you light,
No matter what you're
Going through,
Turn your blues
Into something anew!

The Optimism of the Odds ...Your Perspective Counts!

Isaiah 55:8-9

"For My thoughts are not your thoughts, Nor are your ways My ways," says the Lord. "For as the heavens are higher than the earth, so are My ways higher than yours, and My thoughts than your thoughts," says the Lord. **NKJV**

Think about it...
Perspective - *a point of view or attitude towards something.*
Optimism - *hopefulness/confidence about the success of something.*
Odds (in context) - *difficulties; unpredictable challenges.*

II Samuel 22:32-33

"For who is God except the Lord? And who is a rock, except our God? God is my strength and power, and He makes my way perfect." **NKJV**

As humans–one thing is absolutely sure–we all have different characteristics, thoughts, methods of operating, ideas of living and philosophies about life itself.

In a similar way, our individual perspectives can make or break us within our struggles, pain and problems that we face ever so often. It's so interesting to observe how two or more persons can look at the same painting and conclude surprisingly separate explanations of its meaning.

That's the sheer essence of perspective–the way we see situations whether good or bad reflect our point of view. We all have situations that are negatively mind blowing and physically draining. It may not change overnight or in the blink of an eye, but our outlook can! We have to know what situations and/or circumstances we can work with and which ones we are willing to walk away from. Then truthfully ask yourself–WHY?

When you are stretched outside the realms of your comfort zone, how do you respond? What conclusions do you come with? Defeat or Conquer? Do you saturate yourself

KEDESHA DALLAS GOODE

with the agony of the situation or do you bounce back with a *'go getter,' 'can do,' 'I will bend but I must rise'* attitude?

When your perspective changes positively, you start to engage in responsible thinking; when your perspective is at peace you will let go and let God orchestrate your steps. Life is not free from suffering or pain, but there is a God above who, in His infinite power will work all things together for your good. It's not easy to dismiss the–Why me?–question, likewise it's hard to over arch and underline your thoughts with the fact and knowledge that God through Jesus Christ can do exceedingly abundantly above your problems and burdens. You have to believe it to see it. When your perspective shifts you can praise God through the good and bad times; you can find comfort that nothing lasts forever.

You will begin to mature and grow beyond drowning yourself in worry and wonder. What if life was a bed of roses and all you were exposed to is success and progress without the perils of distress? God's glory would never be revealed, you wouldn't be able to witness the splendor of His superiority. Remember this…God is the author and finisher of our faith; the governor and overseer of our problems. You, me, we are guaranteed safe sailing to the end of our problems because the anchor holds! Our problems may be similar but not identical and that difference is reflective of our perspective. Your perspective can oppose the odds and put some optimism in it.

Sometimes when it seems like all the odds are against you, they are actually for you! When you are at your lowest, the X factor of God's eXtraordinary grace, eXcellent miracles and eXpecting breakthrough is the comfort that we MUST conquer.

The Optimism of the Odds

Obstacles and Odds,
Shackles and prods,
Confused about how to trod,
The road with so many odds,
My God, is there a God?
YES! God already knows,
The suppose and your woes,
The weakness and pain,
From your head to your toes,
The stress and drain,
From the problems and foes.
How will you proceed?
A shift in perspective,
Is what you need!
It will drop you to your knees,
To put a praise on it,
Put God in the midst of it,
Face it, brave it.
Claim the win, sustain your grin,
In the midst of life's grim.
Hold on to your strength
From within,
Opt out of the odds,
With a consistent and
Optimism nod.
Yes you won, Thank God!

KEDESHA DALLAS GOODE

Forgotten in Your Fight ...
But ... Fixed Up for Faith!

Isaiah 43:2
When you pass through the waters, I will be with you; and through the rivers, they shall not overflow you. When you walk through the fire, you shall not be burned, nor shall the flame scorch you. **NKJV**

Think about it…
Fighter - *Someone who does NOT give up; someone who continues fighting or trying.*
FAITH - *is (really) hoping for something that you cannot see.*

Psalm 37:5
Commit your way to the Lord, trust also in Him and He shall bring it to pass. **NKJV**

Romans 8:18
For I consider that the sufferings of this present time are not worthy to be compared with the glory which shall be revealed in us. **NKJV**

Have you ever felt like you're fighting a losing battle? Are you on the brink of breaking? Or are you impatiently blinking for a breakthrough? Either way many times as you go through the bumps and bruises of life, you tend to feel an overwhelming emotion that God must have forgotten you! In your mind, it just seems like your prayers didn't even reach to God's ears. Instead, they have flown over Him. No way! Best believe that He is omnipotent and omnipresent!

It's funny how He knows what we want and when we want it, the tricky part is that we are (most times) over fighting and over exhausting ourselves and then become very distracted. Delay does NOT mean denial. God isn't seemingly ignoring you to ill-treat you. He is actually waiting for the right moment (which is not defined by your timeline) to ignite your best self for His kingdom.

i. Out of Calamity, a Champion is born! When God puts you through some rigorous, tedious and painstaking situations, He's simply churning you to be a champion. To be a champion, you have to see the bigger picture; you have to come to the realization that endurance and resilience are built through hardships. Fear is forgotten when you tap into your faith and trust the process.

ii. My situation is a GRUMP, but I'm growing through every BUMP! Do you realize that after you've gone through an unlikely circumstance attached to a situation, your knowledge of dealing with the bumps of your burden becomes less and less strenuous? It dawned on me that we are unknowingly weak until a truly difficult situation "puzzles" and "punishes" us into thinking that we are unlucky, unthought of or maybe unworthy of anything good. Little did we know that any hard situation is simply growing our grit and rigor so that we are equipped, re-equipped and over equipped to handle anything that hampers our success. Don't focus on the less in the lesson, set your eyes on the promotion of your persona.

iii. God works you to reward you; He exercises you to favour you! Some hardships seem like punishment, some battles seem like a non-stop beating. SIMPLY PUT...it is not your will, but God's will be done. The sooner you accept that fact, the sooner you let go and let God totally govern your affairs. It's no secret that it is really hard to not be in total control of your own affairs, but we are not qualified to 'run our own show.' God is more than cognizant of our desires and He will fulfill them according to His direction. Trust His faithfulness!

iv. The Failure you see in your Fight is Fixing you up for something BIGGER! Purpose + Practice + Push = POWER. Did you know that you are more powerful than you know? All you need is your purpose to be clearly defined, practice good habits that will result in excellence and consistently push to overcome inevitable challenges and obstacles.

KEDESHA DALLAS GOODE

From Fighter to Faith Fanatic

Determined to make it,
Comes what may,
Determined to stay the course,
Even in the face of a delay.
You fight the good fight,
Determined to make your own way, It's not your way!
Didn't you know that God,
Dictates the night & day.
In your furious fight,
You cry out – May Day, May Day
Your anchor gave way!
God? Didn't you hear me pray?
Why did You delay? I wanted my own way,
My way! My Way!
Don't get irate during your wait,
His plans aren't designed
To lead you astray.
He promises major increase for your multiple decrease.
Fervent faith never grows old,
It soothes your aching soul,
It magnifies God's miracles,
In the face of all your obstacles.
Fight to keep your faith,
Stay humble during your wait.

EMPOWERMENT CONVERSATIONS

KEDESHA DALLAS GOODE

Prepared for the Promise? Or Plagued by the Problems?

John 1: 1-5
In the beginning was the word, and the word was with God, and the word was God. He was in the beginning with God. All things were made through Him, and without Him nothing was made that was made. In Him was life, and the life was the light of men. And the light shines in the darkness and the darkness did not comprehend it. **NKJV**

Think about it…
Promise - *A declaration or assurance that one will do something or that a particular thing will happen. Word; guarantee; oath; bond!*
Problem - *unwelcome or unwanted situations that may seem harmful and dangerous.*

Romans 8:31
What then shall we say to these things? If God is for us, who can be against us? **NKJV**

"A promise is a comfort to a fool" as the old proverb dissuades the excitement of a promise, we, as humans can't help but love to be promised something especially when we want it–*inexplicably*–bad. To hold on to a promise that comforts us and gives us hope means that we undoubtedly trust the promisor. Trust is not easy when intertwined with patience. That's because "good things come to those that wait," but who really wants to sit in limbo? Often times when we are told to trust God and hold on to His promises (as outlined in the bible) we shrug at the idea because again our human eye prefers to operate by sight. We'd rather believe what someone says than what the Father promises. Time after time we discover that no man's promise is sure, no man's promise is perfect and no man's promise will totally satisfy. And so… God is the answer. Trust in Jesus, you'll be happy when you accept–not my will but His way!

It's easy to talk about empowerment, motivation and/or inspiration when (it seems) you're not the one with a problem so big, a burden so heavy or a situation so unfortunate. Truth is we are in this struggle together! We are all feeling the blunt of the mental tug-of-war to strengthen our inner man so that our outward actions or life's negative events will not reflect chaos and confusion as well as the fury of FEAR that we face on a daily basis! Don't let your feelings control you! There are no easy answers to trusting God, but what is your next plan of action? Be miserable, live in torment and turmoil; OR trust God to know that you will not and don't have to have the answers because He promised peace and understanding to release anything you can't rectify.

How do you really prepare yourself for God's promises when the problems are so much?! Know what He promises! *'Surely goodness & mercy…Plans to prosper you… Light & your salvation, whom shall I fear…They that wait upon the Lord…'*

Focus on the opportunities of your present and take your eyes off the blunders of your past. God is not like man, He forgives once you confess and desire to grow. Mind your mental wellness; Conform to Transform. Control the cumbersomeness of your mind, that is, the panic and pandemonium. Purposefully conform to positive things and see how your life transforms to attract hope, joy, peace and SUCCESS.

Live your life L.I.T.–Let it go, TOTALLY! Your strength is not sufficient to lift your burdens or bear your heavy loads. God is your refuge and strength. Let go; you cannot control it all.

Respond with the right attitude–try, try and try your best. Not all disappointments or problems require a response of frustration, anger, depression or despair. God is a present help in trouble! Pep yourself up for His promises and push past the problems.

Prepared OR Plagued

Bang, Bang!
The problems smack you like a
Swing song!
Thought you prepared for them,
You dead wrong,
Thought you were strong,
You're not King Kong,
You will be plagued for a while,
But not long.
Soothe your anxiety,
And sing a song,
War through the problems,
Because you're head strong.
Warrior! Survivor! Conqueror!
You're not a rat,
They can't trap your trot,
Rise to the occasion,
And show them what you've got,
Want it so bad, so bad, so bad!
And don't stop,
Believing the promise,
You'll soon rise to the top,
To the top,
To the top,
No stopping that!!

KEDESHA DALLAS GOODE

Anxiety. Doubt. Fear!
Our Extremity is God's
Opportunity.

Jeremiah 32:26-27
Then the word of the Lord came to Jeremiah: "I am the Lord, the God of all mankind. Is anything too hard for me?" **NKJV**

II Corinthians 2:14
Now thanks be to God, which always causeth us to triumph in Christ, and maketh manifest the savour of his knowledge by us in every place. **KJV**

Think about it…
Anxiety + Doubt + Fear - *common factor >THREAT.*
They inflict pain and harm which distorts our mental, physical, emotional and spiritual well being.
God's opportunity - *power to do the undoable.*

Psalm 126:5-6
Those who sow in tears will reap with songs of joy. Those who go out weeping carrying seeds to sow, will return with songs of joy…**NKJV**

    Do you know what it is to fight a battle? I am sure you do! But are you even aware that you are in a daily warfare? Truth be told, we are all in a battle of some kind. Whether it is a clash of thoughts, a struggle of actions, or a confrontation of good and evil–every day we experience some kind of push and pull. The good thing is that we are blessed with the gift of life initiated by waking up to God's new mercies that come with a brand-new day. However, we often times forget this privilege. Instead, we greet the day with the battle of our thoughts; we fight to think meaningfully, we struggle to positively affirm ourselves and we spew complaints that distort our peace. Fact is, when the mind is in a constant battle corrupted by anxiety, doubt and fear, our gateway to goodness is blocked by the threat of the warfare that is in our head. This is completely normal! However, don't think this normalcy is sustainable. No way!

EMPOWERMENT CONVERSATIONS

When the triple threat of anxiety, doubt and fear dictate our modus operandi, best believe that we have lost the battle before it has begun. However, when you are aware of the warfare's objectives, that is: to confuse, disrupt, dishearten and depress YOU, ME and US, it is at this time our high speed thoughts slow to amber and then halts on red. We've stopped because we can't go on, there is a pause in positivity because we've become weary, worrisome and tired. Our efforts are maxed out, our resources are drained and we are on the brink of giving up! WAIT!!!

Our humanness has boundaries but God's power is limitless. When we have gotten to our wits end, it is God's opportunity to show up and show off. It is His chance to make magnificent His might and show us that He does the undoable, specializes in the impossible and can do ANYTHING for His glory. You better believe it! Hands up if sometimes you think and know you can do all things?! Of course we can, BUT! Through Christ who strengthens us.

When all is said and done, God is the beginning and the end. We need Him because there is so much we can do and no more. He is the Governor General, all knowing and all powerful. If we just give Him the opportunity to reveal Himself, we will recognize that our fear is His gear to catapult us to greatness, our doubt is His signal to come through for us in a mighty way, and our anxiety activates His perfect will. Can we depend on God? Yes sir, Yes ma'am!

Yea though we walk through the valley of the shadow of death, God says He is with us. He also assures that *thy rod and thy staff protect me*…When you decide to walk with God and truly commit your life to His order, you'll quickly realize that the battles are hotter but the victories will be sweeter. Don't be scared of the battles, don't run from them. Instead, run towards them and use your God given authority to proclaim–I! Am more than a conqueror; No! weapon formed against me shall prosper; I! am the head and not the tail. Stay in faith. Our weakness is God's greatness.

Anxious but Victorious

Answer me once,
Answer me twice,
Answer me, Oh Lord, because
Waiting isn't always so nice.
I did submit to your will,
I am trying to hold on and be still,
But life's burdens makes a
Mountain out of a molehill.
Most days I am fervent to fight,
Some days I've exhausted all
My might.
I pray day, I pray night,
But! In my eyes,
Things aren't going the way I'd like.
God I know you are there,
Your consistent faithfulness
Shows me that you care.
Lord I know you're working behind the scenes,
I know because I'm surviving
The enemy's plots and schemes.

Lord I know, I know you care,
Send me a sign, some comfort,
So I can see the breakthrough That is near.
Lord, If I cry anymore, I'll lose
Sight of the victory that's in store.
I humbly ask you for more,
More humility, more courage, more of you!
Exceedingly, abundantly above
Is what you do!
It's your will, it's your time,
Because your glory must shine through.
God you promised me your best,
So while you do what I can't do,
Keep me safe to pass this test.
Send me your trusted word to give
My heart some rest.
I bow on my knees,
Not begging you please!
But thanking you for deliverance & grace
With a winning smile on my face
Victory is mine.
Yes Lord you came through right
On time!

Big Dreams! Impossible it Seems. Nothing is Too hard for God ...

Matthew 21:21-22
"Assuredly, I say unto you, if you have faith and do not doubt, you will not only do what was done to the fig tree, but also if you say to this mountain, 'Be removed and be cast into the sea,' it will be done. And whatever things you ask in prayer, believing, you will receive." **NKJV**

Jeremiah 18:6
"O House of Israel, can I not do with you as this potter?" says the Lord. "Look, as the clay is in the potter's hand, so are you in My hand, O house of Israel! **NKJV**

Think about it…

Dreams – *the vision and subsequent belief of an ambition or aspiration that you wish to be materialized in reality.*
Big Dreams – *an amplified vision and subsequent belief of an ambition or aspiration that seems impossible to attain in reality.*

Matthew 4:19-20
And he saith unto them, Follow me, and I will make you fishers of men. And straightaway, they left their nets, and followed him. **KJV**

What is it that you envision? What dreams do you have? Is there a dream so big, so unattainable that you will not let go off its possibility because you believe in its reality? Dreaming is a beautiful vision of something(s) you want to achieve. Believing in that dream is the most important and tedious part of the task because being hopeful of what you cannot see is like a roller coaster emotion of doubt, fear, what ifs and maybes. However, when you believe something, you have to complement that belief with solid and consistent action(s). That action(s) means a concerted and disciplined movement to be mentally in tune with your dreams, physically ready to cease opportunities and emotionally fit to be self-aware of what drives you.

I have been in a situation where I craved a breakthrough so bad that I could actually feel it – that feeling was reflective of my strong belief. Suddenly (and for a brief moment) life's gruesome reality of disappointment stole my dream, and I became withdrawn and despondent, thinking that impossible things are a foregone conclusion. It's ok to feel like this when you have a dream, but it is not ok to operate or stay in this mind set. You will become lifeless and visionless. In my low state, I looked into the mirror, reflected on the (many) blessings I had and used that gratitude to dismiss my solitude and revitalize my fortitude. I sat still, prayed non-stop, tapped into the quiet moments of my heart without the mayhem of the world and I was back on my feet dreaming. I realized my God given power–ACTION, that is, to do something!

My reactivated reckless faith was the compass that directed my action to use my initiative, seek opportunities, be diligent about my objectives and allow God to favor me according to His perfect plan. Dreams fly on wings to unimaginable places and they feed on wholesome mental meals.

We live in a world that has cultured our thoughts and actions to be so much in control that when things don't work according to our vision we get paralyzed into defeat. Or so it seems. We cannot help this feeling because life is so shocking, it's frightening; yet it is so precious leaving you with limitless reasons to persevere in the midst of sporadic scares. When I didn't get my long-awaited breakthrough the way I wanted it or within the time frame I prayed for, I questioned God. Soon, I realized that I was not underserving. Instead, my time wasn't the right time because I had to grow some more, trust God some more and submit to His will. I finally received what I had been praying for–a profession that would allow me to maximize my potential and challenge me to step outside my comfort zone to grow both personally and professionally. I dreamt it. I kept on believing it (with hiccups in between but) alas I received it. Nothing is indeed too hard for God.

Dream. Believe. Receive

Do you have a dream?
Create it! Envision it!
Do you believe in your dream?
Own it! Action it!
How bad to you want to receive your dream?
Claim it! Conquer it!
When you dream,
You visualize the unimaginable,
No matter how unattainable,
God is able to do the impossible.
When you believe,
You activate your faith,
Doubt and fear may speculate,
Sidetrack what your dreams create,
With a long and tedious season of wait.
But! Partake in the wait.
While the wait is not always great,
Don't stumble or shake,
Believe that you have what it takes.
Belief elevates your dream,
To conceive the thought,
Pray for what ought,
To be yours that cannot be bought,
That is a mentally strong mind,
That will action, action and action,
No exception but with dedication,
Dream and Believe the intangible.
To receive the impossible,
From the God of all creation!

KEDESHA DALLAS GOODE

Don't Play it Safe, Find your Place. There is Space!

Judges 6:12
And the angel of the Lord appeared to him, and said to him, "the Lord is with you, you mighty man of valor." **NKJV**

I Peter 2:9
But you are a chosen generation, a royal priesthood, a holy nation, His own special people, that you may proclaim the praises of Him who called you out of darkness into His marvelous light. **NKJV**

***Think about it*…**

Greatness – one's ability and capacity to: recognize their strengths in order to maximize on them; be aware of their weaknesses in order to improve them and tune their efforts to mimic the rhythms of determination, consistency and discipline. Greatness is not bought, it is built…

John 10:10
The thief does not come except to steal and to kill and to destroy. I have come that they may have life, and that they may have it more abundantly. **KJV**

God made you in His likeness and image. Only YOU can determine your greatness. Life is unfair, I know! Life isn't perfect, I am aware! Life is burdensome, I am feeling it! Life is meaningless, I reject it! If we sit and ponder the pandemonium that is taking place all over the world, we will quickly sink ourselves into pity and pain thus seeking greatness in vain. It's time to focus on YOU. What are you made for? What can you do to secure your place in the race to WIN? Winning is not a competition or a comparison. It's an independent mentality to maintain your focus, stay in your lane, improve yourself and ninja through the naysayers. We are all destined to be great and we all have the ability to do great things.

Don't play it safe by being comfortable. Find your place by unlocking your potential and be confident that you can become GREAT too! There is space for all of us. As a young lady seeking to expand my reach for God's glory, I used to get bewildered by life's complexity and my capacity until I grew fully aware of God's grace. Do you know what smacked me in my face, thus removing the cobweb from my space? Learning more about God's faithfulness and experiencing His splendor through numerous breakthroughs.

I now know that I am born with a unique set of gifts and talents that God wants to enlarge for my success and for His glory! I have realized that success is a healthy bowl of soup fuelled and fortified by God as the main ingredient, He is the magic potion and the mouth full of goodness that no one can compete with. God didn't create us to have mediocre lives, instead He created us to WIN; He wants us to break barriers by being exceptionally great at whatever we are called to do. More importantly He requires our total dependence on Him. It's simple, you cannot yearn for success without craving God's intervention. When we trust God to enable us in everyway possible to achieve our highest goals, it is then that we will enjoy and truly bask in success. In the mean time, know that there is (really) only one of you, we all have similarities in the same way we all have a mission to fulfill.

Search your soul for your passion, prick your brain for your purpose, pray to God for His direction and soon you will begin to participate in the pleasure of your mission. Worry less until you worry no more about measuring up to people's standards–create your own in order to fulfill your most impossible goals. What are you willing to change in your life to crank up the volume on WINNING; on becoming better than your disappointments? What will you sacrifice to recalibrate your thinking so that the negative external factors won't be continuously sinking into your being? Drown out distractions with determination; one that will create your space in this race. You can WIN!

Find Your Space ! WIN ...

Life is a winner's race
What does this mean?
Are we on the same team?
Yes, no, maybe so ...
We all have the same dream.
What do you mean?
We want to champion our cause,
But, life's clause will cause
Disappointments and realities to sink its hurtful paws.
Our dreams? Maybe on a little pause, that's normal but,
Keep going because,
You are a winner,
Make haste? No! one pace at a time,
Gets you to the finish line.
Nothing happens too late or too early,
God is always on time!
Secure your space,
With your game face,
Prepare to run a winning race.
Stay focused.
Stay in your lane.
Stay true to you.
Stay faith-FULL.
God will carry you through,
Stay grateful!

KEDESHA DALLAS GOODE

Still Mining your Goals?
It Satisfies your Soul!

Proverbs 3:6

Trust in the Lord with all your heart and lean not on your own understanding; in all your ways submit to him, and he will make your paths straight. **NKJV**

Romans 12:2

Do not conform to the pattern of this world, but be transformed by the renewing of your mind. Then you will be able to test and approve what God's will is–His good, pleasing and perfect will. **NKJV**

Think about it…

A satisfied soul – when your soul relaxes in a space of sweet peace and unwavering inner pleasure it is by virtue of this you know you are soothing a longing for something that will create more consistent discipline that complements motivation.

Goals – an observable or measurable end result of having one or more objectives.

Hebrews 10:35-36

"So do not throw away your confidence; it will be richly rewarded. You need to persevere so that when you have done the will of God, you will receive what he has promised." **NKJV**

---

1. As you enter the last lap of the year, a flood of feelings and emotions maybe causing an unpleasant upset in your stomach thus freezing your flow of thoughts. **YOU ARE STUCK AND STRESSED!**

2. As you recline on the homestretch of the year beaming with hope and acceptance of the big and bountiful blessings you expect, you are overjoyed about your achievements/milestones in the same way you are unbothered about the pests of pessimism. **YOU ARE A SCREAMING SUCCESS!**

3. As you rumble through the rigours of your routine, you are taking things as they come, the end of year fiasco is nothing but a relived rerun that adds to your boring routine. You're a conformist, and there's no zeal to excel or be extraordinary. **YOU ARE A ROUTINE WRECK!**

Which of these scenarios reflect your current state of being? What do you have that makes either scenario fit your life? What are you doing or not doing that makes your chosen scenario the tell-tale of your life?

Woomp Woomp, Yippe Hurray or it's whatever…

Whether the season or occurrences in your life perfectly depict anyone of the scenarios or not, I guarantee that some fragments may duplicate your feelings. If you are on the negative side, don't ride … hop of that train, stop and reroute, it doesn't have to define your destination. As scary as any bad situation may be, ask yourself this: do I have breath/life? What are my losses versus my gains? What is my plan of action?

Stop and take a look into your soul, search yourself and try to figure out what makes you truly happy. Ask yourself what it is that you need that you don't have and start taking disciplined action to achieving your goals at an optimal level. Optimal? Yes! When you want more out of life, seek God's will through Jesus Christ so that you can identify the gifts He has blessed you with. Yes, we ALL have gifts! When you have identified those gifts, you can start to strategize to claim the prize attainable for everyone; you included, that is–**SUCCESS!** Note that real success starts on the inside and is prompted by God's divine ordinance. If you are on the positive side, what is it that you're doing to keep on the firing line?

How will you intentionally continue to blaze the trail for excellence prompted by consistency and staunch determination? When your trajectory is defined by your explicit goals, allow yourself to be sidetracked by change, however do not let it drive fear into you. Just remember that confidently pushing the boundaries of your limits will reflect a rewarding revelation of your soul quenching desires that will leave you floating around in your ability to aim for the highest.

Whatever scenario sits with you at any moment in your life, remember that God will NOT cause you to suffer pain or undergo trials and tribulation beyond your ability. He knows what you can bear! Be patient with yourself while dedicating your dreams to Him so that He will establish your ways according to His will. Pursue your purpose by seeking His direction. Visualize your dreams; work hard towards them. Embrace the pains of the process because, believe me, you have more to gain than to lose.

As an active participant in LIFE, when you have the right attitude and a grateful heart irrespective of your internal feud, the rude and crude realities of your journey will not get ahead of your passion to soothe your soul in pursuit of your God driven goals. Find YOU! Stay true to YOU! Dream big no matter what YOU do! Believe. Believe and hold on to God's words, He promises you will receive!

Go for Goal. Sooth your Soul!

With your goal in plain sight,
Not by your strength but by
His might,
So what's your plight?
Mining your goals,
Sometimes seems like a losing fight.
Fight! that's not right,
Your goals accomplished,
Is what will rubbish
Life's burdensome gibberish,
It's the soul soother,
That makes your day to day
Smoother.
It's a like the perfect garnish,
To a scrumptious dish.
Relish in the journey of going after your goal,
Be bold no matter what you're told
Take control when pessimism
takes a toll,
Identify your goal,
It's the personal satisfaction,
That leads to instant elevation,
What next?
Gratification for the soul,
Before you get old, break the mold,
Satisfy yourself and go for GOLD!

KEDESHA DALLAS GOODE

Are you Eternity Worthy?
Or ... Earthly Sturdy?

John 5:24

Verily truly I tell you, whoever hears my word and believes him who sent me has eternal life and will not be judged but has crossed over from death to life. **NKJV**

Phillipians 3:20-21

But our citizenship is in heaven, And we eagerly await a Savior from there, the Lord Jesus Christ, who, by the power that enables Him to bring everything under His control, will transform our lowly bodies so that they will be like His glorious body. **NKJV**

Think about it...

Eternity - *What is this? Where does one go after death? There must be a place. It cannot just be that they are buried in a grave, skeleton and bones. Full stop!*
Life after death - *Eternity, it can be considered as one's existence after normal life.*

Earth–One of the planets in the solar system that harbors life. Earth is the tangible space of living that we, as humans know ...

John 5: 28-29

Do not be amazed at this, for a time is coming when all who are in their graves will hear his voice and come out–those who have done what is good will rise to live, and those who have done what is evil will rise to be condemned. **NKJV**

Life after death (eternity) is a topic that human's earthly perception and ideas have tried to uncover, explain and unlock. This discovery doesn't reflect any substantial answer instead there are many guesses and theories that lead to common confusion and division. So where are the answers? That leaves us with the only reliable source, the word of God.

The good thing about God's word is that He tells us what life after death is like and He doesn't hide the fact that He IS coming again. As the bible clearly outlines the Lord's second coming, it warns us to get our 'house in order' so that we are ready to face Him as He will display and dissect our earthly duties in order to determine if we lived a life of service to Him through others and in obedience of His words. Did we love our neighbours? Were we fighting every battle carnally? Did we neglect our spirit man and operate solely from our flesh? Did our journey honour God in any way?

How did we make a difference? When we ponder these questions, it can be somewhat scary but it is our reality! God has given us the free will to choose Him and seek salvation. How has that been going? While we may not understand every single thing at all times, God has assured that if we seek Him with all our heart we will find Him, likewise He comforts us with the assurance that He will never leave us nor forsake us. What about those who are not convinced that there is really a God! Well, something or maybe even someone has contributed to that belief.

This belief has led to an increase in segregation of people and contamination of minds where science et al symbolizes the source of our creation. However, followers of Christ have to blaze the trail for the truth that there is only one God. One thing is sure no matter when or how long it takes, the bible highlights that *"every knee shall bow and every tongue will confess that Jesus Christ is Lord"*. If God is love and love is one way to serve God, why is this the hardest thing for us to do, reciprocate, initiate or advocate for?

How can an unbeliever know God through Jesus Christ? How can a believer make an impact?

Welcome to the tell-tale of this journey we call life. As I reflect on the frailty of life, I quickly realize that good and evil prevails oftentimes in the same spaces. There is a constant wrestle–especially in our minds–to choose what to do, when to do it, how to get it done and why is it necessary to do it. The responses to those questions don't

KEDESHA DALLAS GOODE

always–in the first instance–cascade into a response that distinguishes good from evil, most times there is an overlap. The good being what the right thing is and the evil being that inevitable selfish motive that can be either extreme or mere default action. Truth is, when we choose to intentionally operate from a space of doing good and being good we soon realize the peaceful aroma of goodness that engulfs us in a rewarding way.

When I speak of doing something intentionally, it is not a belief system or an attitude that you forge, you cannot be a fraud! When you tap inner (this being of utmost importance) and search deeper you will unlock the truth–love! It is truly an effective tool that releases the burdens of life's bruises and reveals the blessings that we choose to borrow, and most times refuse to OWN! Whether we want to admit it or not, the world was saved by love. ***For God so loved the world that He gave His only begotten son, that whosoever believe in Him will have life and life more abundantly.***

The latter is the challenge we battle with as a people, a nation, and the world. We don't believe in the real love of God and so our earthly duties do not reflect this unconditional love. Instead we are lovers of money and self among many other treacherous traits. How do we qualify to be worthy to enter eternity? Even without thinking, 'worthy,' are our earthly duties reflective of God's love? That is, from an aerial viewpoint–wanting the best for someone at all times no matter what.

Let us endeavour to live in love and most importantly serve God in spirit and truth. Life is short, death is not partial, it doesn't care about our plans or fears. It is an inevitable part of our journey here on earth. So while we are livng and breathing for whatever prescribed time, serve God in spirit and in truth, know him for yourself, study His word and obey His direction.

61

Eternity Worthy or Earthly Sturdy

I know earth is all you know
You were young, now you're grown
Earth is not your home
You won't be left here to roam
There's no forever to treasure
When death whisks you away
All ties you have to sever
What eulogy will they deliver
Did you give into life's guilty pleasure?
Where do you measure
On the ruler's ruler
Are you sturdy
In your earthly duty or
Are you living worthy
To secure your space in eternity
Have you even thought about
Your whereabout
How high have you been bouncing in life's bounce
about, feeling high and mighty

Like you have some amount of clout
Chat bout
Reroute
Get up and shout
It's you Jesus! No doubt
No doubt, no doubt
Life is all about
Jesus, He save us
Jesus, He left the grave for us,
Jesus, He felt the nail for us,
It's a must to put Him 'fus'
Salvation is our outlet
You start fret yet?
Don't fret, just know
with Jesus there's no regret
No regret
Your life seems like a mess?
Jesus is on speed dial
Call upon Him,
He'll give you a reset!

Greatness—one's ability and capacity to: recognize their strengths in order to maximize on them; be aware of their weaknesses in order to improve them and tune their efforts to mimic the rhythms of determination, consistency and discipline. Greatness is not bought, it is built…

Kedesha

Acknowledgements

God's faithfulness continues to be my driving force, I am nothing without Him; He has given me everything -the gifts and talents. I give them back to Him for His glory!

To Maddison, my beloved daughter, you make it easy to love. Your compassion, your smile, your sweet persona and smarts have equated to the beautiful and blessed girl that you are. May the Lord continue to bless you in every way and enlarge your territories for His glory. I love you so much!

To my husband Evon, your support from every angle and in every way is the magnet to motivation and the push to my purpose. Your understanding during my demanding schedule and impulsive engagements, is unmatched. I thank God for you and our team work. I love you Vaughn!

To my mother Hermina, your strength of character is the wind beneath my wings; your consistent encouragement is the rev to my engine. Your love and support are the pep in my step. I thank you Mommy!

To my father and brothers, thanks for finding the value in our valleys. Your support and belief in my dreams are the joyous jolts in my journey. I love you all.

To my supportive circle of friends, I appreciate your belief in me, the continuous prayers, the unwavering love and the ongoing support. I love you and God bless you all.

What else does Kedesha do?

. Empowerment (motivational) speaking and/or coaching.

. Professional and personal Spanish and French language classes for all levels: children, teens & adults.

. Fashion & Graphics - Instagram@hugup_kedesha

Share your reviews, thoughts and comments abut this book on Amazon.

Purchase her other book **Sorrow Soothers: Mind Pleasers & Victory Verses** on Amazon.com

For more information or to get in touch with Kedesha, **send an email to kdallasgoode@gmail.com or via**

www.ingramcontent.com/pod-product-compliance
Lightning Source LLC
Chambersburg PA
CBHW050013040726
47599CB00014B/1359